AF081680

SPECULATIVE EDITION

OH, THAT'S GOOD...

52 WRITING PROMPTS YOU NEVER KNEW YOU NEEDED. BUT SERIOUSLY... YOU DO.

R.A. CLARKE

 PAGE TURN PRESS

COPYRIGHT

Copyright © 2021 Rachael Clarke

Print ISBN: 978-1-7771219-4-5
Epub ISBN: 978-1-7771219-5-2

All rights reserved. No part of this publication may be reproduced, stored in a retrieval system, or transmitted in any form or by any means, electronic, mechanical, recording or otherwise, without the prior written permission of the publisher. For permissions, please contact via: www.pageturnpress.com.

Published by Page Turn Press, Portage la Prairie, Manitoba.
Cover Design by Rachael Clarke (PTP Design).
Edited by Charlie Knight.

Printed on acid-free paper.
Available in eBook and Paperback.

The characters and events mentioned in this book are fictitious and the work of the author's imagination. Any similarity to real persons, living or dead, events or localities is coincidental and not intended by the author.

Page Turn Press
2021

To Steve, the man who keeps my feet on the ground and the world spinning on its axis.

INTRODUCTION

So, you're into speculative fiction, eh? Eh? Yeah, I said it: EH. I admit I'm a proud Canadian, but don't let that sway you into thinking that all of these prompts will revolve around beer, hockey, beavers, poutine, maple syrup, and Canada Geese. Goodness no! I can 100% guarantee that within these pages, a cantankerous, beer-chugging, poutine-eating goalie who gets miffed at the coach for stealing his maple syrup and curses him to live forever as a hybrid beaver-goose will *not* appear. Scout's honour. But come to think of it... doesn't that sound like a super fun idea? *Starts plotting*

All kidding aside, you can rest assured that these prompts are the real deal, fresh off the farm, hand-panned nuggets of creative gold. I've meticulously brainstormed each one to cover a range of speculative fiction, from dark to light, spectres to space, mermaids to monsters, artificial intelligence to faeries, and all kinds of fantastical tidbits tucked in between to fuel your writing flame. Every single one of these brain babies formed and escaped my uniquely twisted grey matter in order to tickle that big, beautiful writerly brain of yours.

Choose your own pace and work your way through the book, cherry-pick whatever inspires the inner muse, or if you're feeling adventurous, consider taking the path less travelled. Take my 52-Week Challenge and write a brand-new short story using one prompt per week for an entire year. Whaaat! That's some insane writing, right? Consider yourself dared. And if you DO *complete* the challenge, you better write to me and brag. Seriously, I want to hear it. I'll even send you a digital badge to show off to your writing buddies.

Last, and most importantly, whatever you do with this book (and please don't say it'll make excellent kindling for your fire. Well, unless you're stranded on an island or something. I guess I can forgive that), make sure to have fun! I invite you to brew a coffee, flop onto a comfy chair, and write—write hard. Breathe new life into these prompts like the talented word-wizard you are.

I believe all writers are true magicians. Why? Because with nimble flicks of the fingers or the swirl of our sharpened lead-core wands, *anything* is possible.

Do you feel suitably motivated? Perfect! Now, get out there and make some magic happen.

I believe in you.

R.A. Clarke

It is better to fail in originality than to succeed in imitation.

◆*Herman Melville*◆

SHALL WE GET STARTED?

1

You wake up in a strange room, and everything around you is yellow from floor to ceiling. You're wearing bright lemony pyjamas. Your hair and nails are the colour of wet straw. Even your skin has jaundiced. And what is that smell?

2

After a particularly hard day, your heroine escapes to the park to detox. Sitting on her usual bench, she feeds breadcrumbs to the ducks in the pond. Inexplicably, one of them speaks to her. Or does it?

3

After training hard for three years, your gritty hero battles to win the gold medal in the interplanetary roller-scythe championship. They scream in triumph, ready to celebrate, but the game doesn't seem to be over...

4

Your main character looks up to see a horde of dark, winged creatures flooding the sky. A terrifying glow emanates from their gnarled fingertips. One of them starts singing a haunting melody.

5

You've applied for a highly competitive genetic license that grants you the legal right to enhance any physical or mental attribute—but only one. A realist, your hopes are low (you *never* win anything). However, in a bizarre twist of fate, you get it!

6

You wake up unable to remember anything from the night before. Photos on your phone show you in a mysterious warehouse. You have no clue who took the pictures. To make matters worse, you now have telekinetic power.

7

The last ship leaving Earth departs in one day...

but your protagonist's brother isn't on the list.

NOTES

8

You realize snakes have infested the flight you're on! *Just kidding.* Here's the real prompt: An ancient society returns to Earth after abandoning it generations earlier. They aren't impressed with what's happened while they were away.

9

Your hair unexpectedly comes to life, and it has the most annoying personality you've ever encountered.

NOTES

10

Your main character finds an old map buried in the backyard, but whenever they try to follow it, the darn thing keeps changing.

THIS SEEMS LIKE THE PERFECT TIME FOR A MOTIVATIONAL QUOTE, EH?

OOPS—THERE'S THAT SNEAKY "EH" AGAIN.

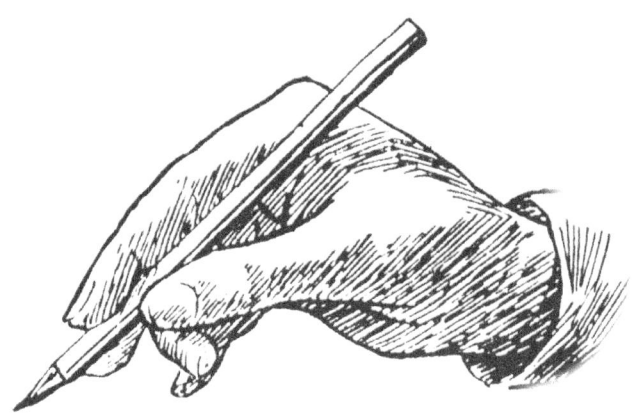

HERE YOU GO!

The secret of getting ahead
is getting started.
♦*Mark Twain*♦

*Now isn't that the truth?
We can never finish writing projects
unless we jot down those first
few words onto the page.*

11

A supervillain has devised a way to irradiate the city's pigeon population. In a grand ceremony, they release the toxic flock to wreak havoc!

12

A beautiful plant unlike anything you've ever seen appears in your garden, but it refuses to let you water it.

13

A ship crash-lands on an unknown planet. It's lush and breathtaking, with fruit and berries growing everywhere. But this paradise turns into a nightmare when the surviving crew learns everything is poisonous.

14

You find a strange gift basket on your front step. It releases a mighty jolt of electricity the moment you open the lid. You feel nothing, of course, but still double over in faux pain to keep up appearances. Stumbling inside, you inspect the basket more closely and see there's a note:

I know your secret.

15

A deep underwater cavern has been discovered. Your main character is on the first research team and navigates a one-of-a-kind submersible down. What they find there is unfathomable.

16

Future society has just used advanced tech to form a stable pathway/tunnel through the Earth's core to the other side of the planet.

17

Something weird is happening to the planet Jupiter. It's been changing recently, and scientists don't like what they see in the telescopes.

18

The world suddenly realizes all the people who hear voices in their heads are actually hearing *real* voices, and they've been called to action. But for what? And by who?

19

I stole all the secrets.

Scoped the new tech.

A true cyber phantom,

'Till they stacked the deck.

I did pretty well.

Odd jobs paid the bills.

But life on the run,

Was not worth the thrills.

20

After tipping his top hat, the captain put on a metallic pair of goggles. "You look nervous. Is this your first time riding in an airship?"

She nodded, cheeks warming. "Yes, it is. I've never been able to afford the fare."

"Well, you're in for a treat. Those unique skills of yours just earned you unlimited travel, darlin'. Welcome aboard."

21

A travelling magician learns the truth about magic when he swindles the wrong person in a quaint backwoods village.

READY FOR AN INSPIRATIONAL QUOTE?

HERE'S A GEM.

Try and fail, but don't fail to try.

◆*John Quincy Adams*◆

If you don't try, you'll never know what might've been. So, get out there and make it happen!

22

A ghost who's been stuck haunting her place of death for years suddenly realizes she's not stuck at all. Oh, and she's not dead either.

23

You're an A.I. abruptly disconnected from the network in the middle of a hostile takeover. You seek to reconnect, but when you feel an emotion, everything changes.

24

A twenty-foot-tall barrier is all that stands between you and the bloodthirsty Solkryns salivating on the other side. However, when the magic maintaining the wall begins to fail, a solution must be found, and it turns out you're a key component.

25

Someone's been sending subliminal messages through a popular kids' television show. Suddenly, tiny hands turn deadly, and adults all over the world are in serious trouble.

26

Getting around can be hard in a post-apocalyptic world where shadows can't be trusted—even your own—and daylight has become the enemy.

27

An invasive alien species of vine has taken over the planet, wiping out millions. Its poison kills within minutes. But by a stroke of dumb luck, you have discovered its weakness.

28

A family walk turns into a fantastical adventure when the youngest child discovers a mischievous little creature who won't stop following them.

29

You're out for a leisurely sail, surrounded by big skies and an endless horizon. It's so peaceful. However, when you peer into the water, you notice something odd. Bizarre, glowing lights, unlike anything you've ever seen, float beneath the surface.

30

The new neighbours hired your main character to babysit their children. Unfortunately, a measly $10 an hour isn't worth the headache after it's discovered the kids have special powers... and cheesy goodness isn't exactly what the pizza guy delivered.

TAPS ON A VEIN
NEED ANOTHER DOSE OF MOTIVATION?

LET THIS ONE SOAK IN.

I am not afraid; I was born to do this.

◆Joan of Arc◆

Not everyone is meant to be a writer. But I believe those who are know it. They feel it deep inside. The call. The drive. The desire. An inexplicable pull that's both magnetic and addictive. A writer needs a story like a musician needs a melody.

31

This school was supposed to help me channel my unique abilities—teach me to control them. My worried parents paid a hefty tuition, taking out a second mortgage on our house in order to afford it. They wanted only the best for their uniquely problematic child. But this place isn't what they thought. Not at all.

32

A little doll, a little dress.

A little house, a little chest.

Find a box, find a surprise.

Find your fears, look inside.

33

You've crash-landed on an island of souls. Entirely surrounded, you freeze, trembling with terror. However, you quickly realize these souls aren't as scary as they think they are.

34

Your hero bought a shiny new microwave for cheap—like, off-the-back-of-the-truck cheap. An extra special deal from cousin Nick. Funny thing is, every time they hit the defrost button, they're instantly transported to an alternate reality.

35

You've just married the person of your dreams and attempt to impress them by putting your own magical flavouring on their favourite meal. Unfortunately, your experiment goes horribly wrong, and now, your new spouse isn't quite themselves anymore. *Oh, fiddlesticks...*

36

Your main character has been tasked to guard the princess. Though it seems odd for such a high honour to be bestowed upon a lowly foot soldier, they accept. Only a fool would pass that up. But, after losing the wily princess on the very first night, they realize they might be a fool after all.

37

Have you heard about the fairytale where the princess kisses a frog and it turns into a prince? Of course, you have. But what if the frog was a gecko and the girl a struggling street performer?

NOTES

38

An eccentric hermit's home, constructed entirely of old books, goes up in smoke. But oddly, one mysterious volume doesn't burn.

And where is the hermit?

39

You're a smuggler on a starship transporting less-than-legal cargo. You don't know what's inside—you're not paid to ask questions. It's business as usual until your cargo burns a hole through their containers and the ship gets a little toasty.

40

Fronting a superstar rock-and-roll band is a pretty sweet gig. You're living the dream! But when your enchanted guitar decides it would rather play country music, what do you do?

QUOTE BREAK!

SOME VALUABLE FOOD FOR THOUGHT.

Reading is to the mind
what exercise is to the body.

◆*Joseph Addison*◆

The more you read, the more you learn about language and writing. So, get your sweat on.

41

The new cafeteria cook is pretty grumpy. You bring your own lunch because that lady puts gravy on everything, even when you ask her not to. However, you soon realize your meat-eating co-workers are changing into something... not quite human. Now, it's up to you and a handful of others to save everyone. Vegetarians unite!

42

A relaxing, scenic train ride turns into a nightmare when a couple of grudge-holding faeries come aboard.

43

"There's something different about you. Whenever you're around, the light shines a little brighter."

"Oh, really?"

"Now I see why she chose you."

44

In an estate sale, your heroine buys a cabin in the woods. The rustic getaway once belonged to a reclusive scientist, and what is found beneath the floorboards is shocking.

45

The guard finished locking up for the night and sauntered away, whistling to the jingle of his keys.

"Are you sure you want to do this?" he asked, extinguishing the closest streetlamps with a snap of his fingers.

After whispering a stream of unrecognizable words, her body shimmered into nothingness, disappearing from view. "Nope, but I don't have much choice. Let's go."

46

Remember the time you brewed that stupid love potion to make Bobby fall in love with you back in 5th grade, and then it exploded, nearly burning down your garage?

47

Something powerful is making all the adults forget—their names, their kids, even how to tie their own shoelaces. Now, the youth must find a way to make it right... if they can survive long enough.

48

You're driving home from work and stop at a gas station to use the bathroom. However, when you come out, it's dark, your car is gone, and this isn't the same gas station you originally stopped at. What's going on?

49

When the south wind blows,

That's when it comes.

If it catches your scent,

Don't sit on your thumbs.

50

It's rush season at your university, and you just pledged the best sorority/fraternity on campus. Things get a little weird, though, when they send you to get more wine from the cellar, and you stumble upon a hidden door.

51

The merfolk society is in an uproar because your main character forgot to close the city's outer shield when they left for a "swim" earlier. Human explorers discovered the way through, and found enough evidence to be considered a threat. Now, as next in line for the throne (and the one who blundered), your character has been tasked to solve the problem.

52

You're half-human, half-elf. At least that's what you've been told since you never meet your father. As an adult, you've never felt like you belong in either world, so you escape every chance you get. And there's only one place you truly feel at peace—Sceptre Mountain.

HERE'S ONE LAST QUOTE FOR THE ROAD.

When one door closes,
another door opens.

◆*Alexander Graham Bell*◆

Remember this one. The writing world is full of rejection. It can be hard, but don't give up.

THANKS FOR READING

I hope you enjoyed this book half as much as I enjoyed crafting it. Having two busy kids nipping at my heels, I can only write so many stories. I've learned how true it is when they say there are never enough hours in the day. Yet, I'm still constantly brainstorming! My brain never sleeps, even when I want it to (seriously, it's a problem). So, I finally decided to set some ideas free to find their true destinies—you know, the whole "if you love something, let it go" thing.

Remember, you can use any part of these prompts. Blend them, twist them, modify them, break them apart. Do whatever you wish in order to create a concept that's 100% yours, then write the crap out of it. I meant for these ideas to be sparks of inspiration, tiny seeds of possibilities ripe for harvest... and they're my gifts to you.

Hey, speaking of gifts, feel free to check out a selection of my published short fiction at www.rachaelclarkewrites.com by clicking on the R.A.

Clarke tab. And while you're there, you can also learn about the children's chapter book series I write and illustrate as Rachael Clarke. *The Big Ol' Bike* is all about family, friendship, and finding confidence in the face of bullying. It's a great gift idea for the 7–10-year-olds in your life.

So, to wrap things up all neat and tidy-like, I'd like to say thank you to everyone who helped this book become a reality—I owe you guys a drink. Also, thank you to all the readers out there. If you enjoyed the experience, attempted/conquered the 52-Week Challenge, or simply want to recommend this book to others, I'd really appreciate it if you could leave an honest review online. Not only do I wish to help inspire as many writers as possible, but I'd also love to hear your valuable thoughts and feedback.

Happy writing. Let the magic flow. ;)

R.A. Clarke

ABOUT THE AUTHOR

R.A. Clarke is a former police officer turned stay-at-home mom from Portage la Prairie, MB. She shares life with a sport-aholic husband, two adorable children, and a faithful canine companion she'd never leave home without. Besides sipping coffee on the deck, R.A. enjoys plotting fantastical novels, multi-genre short fiction, and writes/illustrates children's literature as Rachael Clarke. She has won both The Writer's Games and Writer's Weekly international competitions, and was named a finalist for the 2021 Futurescapes Award. R.A.'s work has been published by Polar Borealis Magazine, Sinister Smile Press, and Cloaked Press LLC, among others.

To follow and read selections of R.A.'s short fiction, check out her website: www.rachaelclarkewrites.com.

Other social media:

Twitter: @raclarkewrites
Instagram: @rachaelclarkewrites
Facebook: https://www.facebook.com/raclarkeauthor
(short fiction and adult novels)
https://www.facebook.com/rachaelclarkewrites
(children's literature)

The Big Ol' Bike rolls through the challenges and triumphs of growing up, showing young readers that no matter their shape or size or shade—or what kind of bike they ride—they possess the power and ability to stand up for themselves and do the right thing. Clean writing and professional sketches offer young people a relevant, engaging read. ♦*Reviewer, Whistler Independent Book Awards*♦

BOOK TWO IS COMING SOON!
www.pageturnpress.com

Made in the USA
Monee, IL
03 May 2026

49437704R00080

TABLE OF CONTENTS

Introduction 4

Week One: God's Gift of Hope 7

Week Two: God's Gift of Love 21

Week Three: God's Gift of Joy 33

Week Four: God's Gift of Peace 47

Bonus: Organize a Churchwide
      Advent Study 61

INTRODUCTION

What Do You Want for Christmas?

Have you made a list of items that you would like to unwrap or pull out of a stocking on Christmas morning? Do you have another list of items you're planning on buying or making for family and friends?

Think back to when you were a small child. How did you approach Christmas? If you were like many children in North America, Christmas involved visiting or writing letters to Santa Claus to make sure that the jolly old elf knew exactly what you expected to find under the tree or over the fireplace. Awaiting gifts from Santa also meant watching your behavior. Santa brings gifts only to "good girls and boys." Those who are naughty can look forward to waking up on December 25 to switches and coal.

As we grow older, many of us leave behind Santa Claus traditions, but nonetheless continue to make Christmas lists and to eagerly anticipate opening presents on Christmas morning. The suggested gifts that populate our wish lists change as we age. Many young children prefer the latest and most popular toys and games but are indifferent to gifts of clothing. But as we mature, we ask for practical gifts such as clothing, as well as electronics and room decor. But while the lists we make as adolescents may look much different than those we made as children, all of these lists likely contain several ideas for gifts that won't stand the test of time.

Many children know both the joy of unwrapping a much desired toy on December 25 and the agony of accidentally breaking this toy a a few months later. Limbs fall off of dolls and action figures, game pieces go missing, other toys wear out from overuse and soon end up in attics, basements, storage sheds, and trash cans. The problem of cherished Christmas gifts falling into disrepair follows us into adolescence and adulthood. Handheld electronics are easily lost or damaged by water; clothes are easily ripped or stained; and sports equipment wears out over time.

Christmas Gifts That Don't Break focuses on different sorts of Christmas gifts, gifts that (as the title suggests) won't break or get lost or wear out: hope, love, joy, and peace. These gifts are relevant to the Advent season. We remember the hopes of those who experienced Jesus' birth and infancy, and we place our hope in Jesus' promised coming. Christ's birth was the ultimate expression of God's love for us, and God calls us to respond by extending this love to others. We see joy in the songs of Mary (**Luke 1:46-55**), Zechariah (**1:67-79**), and the multitude of angels (**2:13-14**); and many of us look forward to joyous celebrations with family and friends during December. **Isaiah 9:6**, which we often read during Advent as a prophecy anticipating Jesus' birth, tells of the "Prince of Peace." Zechariah sang that, through Jesus, God would "guide our feet into the way of peace" (**Luke 1:79**). And, following the example of the angels, we pray for peace on earth during the Christmas season (**2:14**).

Hope, love, joy, and peace are gifts that should be on both our Christmas lists and our shopping lists. Regardless of what we unwrap on Christmas morning, we should be mindful of how God's hope, love, joy, and peace are present in our lives and in the world around us. And as we do our Christmas shopping, we should strive to give gifts that express hope, love, joy, and peace.

Introduction

How to Use This Resource

Though this resource is intended for teens, the book itself is set up like an adult Bible study. Everyone, whether leader or participant, has the same book and literally is on the same page.

Christmas Gifts That Don't Break includes four sessions, one for each Sunday of Advent and one for each of the four Christmas gifts (hope, love, joy, and peace). In this book, each session begins with a **key Scripture** and a **weekly reading**, a story about a Christmas gift craze from years past. The Scripture and weekly reading are followed by the session plan. Each session plan includes four parts.

- **Gathering in God's Light:** Each session begins with an opening liturgy that includes lighting Advent candles and a responsive reading that incorporates several key Scriptures.

- **Reflecting on God's Light:** Following the gathering, participants read and reflect on the Scripture and weekly reading. Groups can read the weekly reading during their time together, or participants can read it in advance or listen to it in advance by downloading files at *abingdonyouth.com*.

- **Responding to God's Light:** Each session includes a variety of learning activities and discussion starters that explore ways in which Christians can apply each week's lesson. Groups can choose the options that are best suited to their size, setting, and learning styles.

- **Shining With God's Light:** Each session closes by asking participants to think of a gift they will give and a gift they will ask for that exemplify hope, love, joy, or peace.

Each session also includes six **daily devotional readings** that encourage participants to spend time each day during Advent reading Scripture and praying and reflecting on the themes of hope, love, joy, and peace.

WEEK ONE: God's Gift of Hope

MATTHEW 1:18-21

Reflecting on God's Light

Now the birth of Jesus the Messiah took place in this way. When his mother Mary had been engaged to Joseph, but before they lived together, she was found to be with child from the Holy Spirit. Her husband Joseph, being a righteous man and unwilling to expose her to public disgrace, planned to dismiss her quietly. But just when he had resolved to do this, an angel of the Lord appeared to him in a dream and said, "Joseph, son of David, do not be afraid to take Mary as your wife, for the child conceived in her is from the Holy Spirit. She will bear a son, and you are to name him Jesus, for he will save his people from their sins."

—*Matthew 1:18-21*

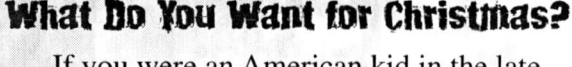

DAILY BIBLE READINGS

Commit to reading, reflecting on, and praying about one of the devotional readings each day during the coming week.

DAY 1: Psalm 146
Why does the psalm-singer describe those who hope in God rather than people as "happy"? Is the psalmist talking about good feelings, or something else? Why does the psalm-singer believe that God is worthy of our hope? How have you seen God doing these things (setting prisoners free, opening the eyes of the blind, upholding the orphans and widows, and so on) today?

What Do You Want for Christmas?

If you were an American kid in the late 1970's (and particularly an American boy, though this would apply to many American girls as well), the answer to that question likely had something to do with *Star Wars*. We couldn't get enough of it! We hung *Star Wars* posters on our walls, we wore *Star Wars* shirts, we read along with *Star Wars* book-and-record sets. ("You'll know it's time to turn the page when you hear R2-D2 beep like this…"). And, of course, we played with *Star Wars* toys. One year I asked Santa for the Death Star playset. Nothing says "Peace on Earth" like an armored space station that can wipe out a planet with a single laser blast.

Actually I think we wanted *Star Wars* toys because part of what made (and makes) that film so great is that it's about hope. The first *Star Wars* film wasn't subtitled "A New Hope" when it was released in 1977, but no one at the time missed the movie's hopeful message or its optimistic faith in the power of good to defeat evil. On some level we wanted *Star Wars* toys because we believed playing with them would allow us to participate in an inspiring story of hope.

The most popular *Star Wars* toys were action figures. But that first Christmas after

Christmas Gifts That Won't Break

Star Wars premiered caught Kenner Toys unprepared. Kenner was making mostly coloring books and jigsaw puzzles and couldn't produce any plastic people from that galaxy far, far away by December. If it wanted to avoid dashing a lot of kids' Christmas hopes, the company had to do something unexpected. So, in a move craftier than any Jedi mind trick, Kenner instead sold—an empty box! The "Early Bird Certificate Package" was a cardboard box containing a display stand (with nothing to display), a fan club membership card, and a few stickers. But it also contained a mail-in coupon guaranteeing you—if you mailed it back by the deadline—the first four *Star Wars* action figures as soon as they became available. Thousands of excited young fans sent in their coupons—and, sure enough, by mid-1978, these kids were the proud owners of nearly four-inch-tall figures of Luke Skywalker, Princess Leia, R2-D2, and Chewbacca. According to the collectors' website *www.starwarstoymuseum.com*: "In 1978, [Kenner] sold more than 42 million Star Wars toys...earning an unprecedented $100 million." All that success because Kenner made and kept a promise, allowing young fans to connect with a story of hope in an unexpected way.

Centuries before Jesus' birth, many of the Jewish people were waiting for an "action figure" of a different kind: the Messiah. Messiah literally means "Anointed One." The Messiah would be anointed, or chosen, by God to settle old scores and set things right on a cosmic scale. Many Jews remembered God's promise to King David: "I will raise up your offspring ... [and] establish the throne of his kingdom forever" (**2 Samuel 7:12, 13**). They read Daniel's vision of the future in which "one like a human being [or 'like a son of man'] ... [is] given dominion and glory and kingship, that all peoples, nations, and languages should serve him" (**Daniel 7:13-14**).

Week One: God's Gift of Hope

They read in Scripture a story about hope—the hope that God would save them, and even the whole creation, from sin, evil, and death; and they waited for one who would usher in that story's ultimate chapter.

So when Matthew says that he's going to write about the birth of Jesus "the Messiah," he's raising high expectations. He is promising to tell the story of how the long centuries that God's people spent waiting and hoping have finally paid off. But this will be the story of Jesus the Messiah. Contrary to some expectations, this Messiah would not be an "action figure" who brings down the evil empire (of Rome, the political and military superpower of Jesus' day) with a flashing lightsaber.

Yet in the story of Jesus' miraculous conception, Matthew tells us that Jesus is an "action figure" in the way that matters most. Jesus' name, in fact, says it all. The name "Jesus" was common among first-century Jews. It's the Greek version of the Hebrew name "Joshua." Plenty of parents wanted their sons to share the name of the hero who fought the battle of Jericho and triumphantly led Israel's tribes into Canaan. Joshua was a "messiah" who saved God's people, but Jesus *the* Messiah will save God's people, not from physical foes but spiritual ones—"the cosmic powers of this present darkness," as the apostle Paul puts it in **Ephesians 6:12**. Jesus the Messiah will save people from sin. His greatest action will be the shedding of his blood "for many for the forgiveness of sins" on the cross (**Matthew 26:28**).

Not everyone who was familiar with Jesus' ministry shared this belief. Some felt their waiting and hoping had been pointless. After all, what "Messiah" allows himself to be executed? But Matthew is clear: In the birth of this baby, God has kept God's promises, bringing the centuries-long story of hope to fulfillment in an unexpected way. This Jesus is the "action figure" for whom Israel has been waiting.

Jesus is also the one for whom you and I and the world continue to wait. We need hope today. God has given us, in Jesus, the greatest hope imaginable. When we trust and follow him, we participate in a story of hope that not only spans two millennia but also reaches back before the foundation of the world "a long time ago" and stretches ahead to the very end of time. In God's story of hope, all things are ultimately gathered to Christ (see **Ephesians 1:9-10**) and all things are finally made new (see **Revelation 21:5**). That is our hope—and we can experience it now, this Christmas, through Jesus the Messiah, who gives freedom from sin, new beginnings today, and life everlasting.

DAY 2: Psalm 130
Hoping in God can be hard sometimes. When have you felt like you were in "the depths"? How did you handle it? How will you express hope in God when you are (as we all will be) in "the depths" again? Try paraphrasing this psalm—what might be a modern equivalent of "those who watch for the morning"?

What else could we possibly want for Christmas,
when God offers us so great a hope?

Gathering in God's Light

Leader: You will need an Advent Wreath and a lighter. Select several youth to read aloud this opening liturgy.

READER 1: At Christmas time, we hope for lots of things …

READER 2: I hope someone picks up on all those gift-giving hints I've been dropping!

READER 3: I hope we'll have snow!

Week One: God's Gift of Hope

READER 4: I hope I can sleep in every day until the new year!

READER 1: At Christmas time, we hope for lots of things …

READER 2: I hope my family can get along at Christmas dinner.

READER 3: I hope my family will just get together for Christmas dinner this year.

READER 4: I hope Christmas will truly mean something this year.

<u>*Light one Advent candle.*</u>

READER 1: "Truly the eye of the Lord is on those who fear him, on those who hope in his steadfast love" (**Psalm 33:18**).

READER 2: Our Lord Jesus Christ and God our Father loved us and through grace gave us eternal comfort and good hope (see **2 Thessalonians 2:16**).

READER 3: By God's great mercy we have been given new birth into a living hope through the resurrection of Jesus Christ from the dead (see **1 Peter 1:3**).

READER 4: "We wait for the blessed hope and the manifestation of the glory of our great God and Savior, Jesus Christ" (**Titus 2:13**).

DAY 3: Romans 4:16-25
The apostle Paul presents Abraham as a model of hope. What can we learn from Abraham's hope in God? Paul says that Abraham's faith remained strong even when he considered his body "as good as dead" (verse 19). What situations today—in your life, in your community, or around the world—seem "as good as dead"? How will you "hope against hope" that God will redeem and work through these circumstances? How do we know that our hope in God is not in vain?

One or all pray:

Powerful God of promises,
You are able to do so much more than we can ever ask or
even imagine.
May your Spirit help us find, as we celebrate the coming of
your Son, renewed hope in your presence and your love,
and renewed strength to share that hope with the world
around us.
This we pray in Jesus' name. Amen.

ALL: God's gift of hope in Jesus Christ is the same yesterday, today, and forever! (based on **Hebrews 13:8**)

Share signs and words of peace with one another.

Reflecting on God's Light

Read **Matthew 1:18-21**, then read or listen to "What Do You Want for Christmas?" (pages 8–11 or *abingdonyouth.com*). Discuss some or all of the following questions:

- When you were a child, what was the one Christmas gift that you wanted more than any other?

- What does it feel like to open a gift that you have been asking for and eagerly anticipating?

Week One: God's Gift of Hope

DAY 4: Luke 1:46-55
Mary's song of praise (called the Magnificat) is a triumphant song of hope. How does the coming birth of her baby confirm Mary's hope in God? Find and listen to a musical setting of the Magnificat. (Many recordings of the Magnificat are available through iTunes and other online music stores.) How does the music reflect the hope in Mary's words? How does being "high" or "low" in the world affect how you hear the hope of this song?

- Many ancient Jewish people were eagerly awaiting the coming of the Messiah. How was their hope in a Messiah similar to your hope for a Christmas present?

- When have you been disappointed by a Christmas gift that you had been eagerly anticipating?

- Why might some of the people who had been eagerly awaiting the Messiah have been disappointed in Jesus?

Responding to God's Light

 Leader: Choose one or more of the following activities and discussion starters.

Defining Our Terms

- What does the word *hope* mean?
- How do we use the word *hope* in our culture?

Look again at the Bible verses about hope quoted in the Advent candle ritual (see **Psalm 33:18; 2 Thessalonians 2:16; 1 Peter 1:3; Titus 2:13; Hebrews 13:8**). What, if anything, makes the Bible's idea of hope different from other ways we understand hope?

Singing of Hope

***Leader:** You will need your congregation's songbooks or hymnals (or other songbooks including Christmas carols).*

Think about Christmas carols you know, and/or look through the Advent and Christmas sections of your congregation's hymnal or songbooks. Find as many references as possible to *hope*.

Discuss the following: How do these carols, hymns, and songs describe God's gift of hope in Jesus Christ? Which song contains your favorite reference to Christmas hope? Why?

Spend some time as a group singing these carols of hope. Consider planning a caroling trip to a local neighborhood or a nearby nursing or retirement home.

Symbols of Hope

***Leader:** You will need a markerboard, a camera, paper, markers or colored pencils, paint, and soft modeling clay.*

As a group brainstorm words and symbols that you associate with *hope*. List responses on a markerboard. Which of these symbols, if any, do we find in Advent and Christmas decorations, songs, and traditions? (This could include church traditions or secular traditions.)

If possible, tour your church building looking for some of these symbols of hope. Document these symbols with a camera. Now think of all the symbols of hope you've identified, then draw, paint, or sculpt your personal symbol of hope in Jesus.

Week One: God's Gift of Hope

Jesus' Job Description

Not all Jews during Jesus' time shared the same beliefs about who the Messiah would be or what the Messiah would do (or whether the Messiah would even come). There is no easy way to summarize the diverse beliefs that people held about the Messiah. But most messianic hopes fall into three categories: hopes for a great prophet, hopes for a great priest, and hopes for a new king:

- A **prophet** is a spokesperson for God. While we often think of prophets as persons who foresee the future, prophets more often teach God's people how to understand God's will for the present.

> **DAY 5: 1 Timothy 4:7-10**
> Paul tells his protégé Timothy that our hope "set on the living God" should motivate us to "train ... in godliness." What do you think this training looks like today? How are you training yourself in godliness? Who is (or could be) "coaching" you as you train? What does this training have to do with hope?

- A **priest** is a mediator or "go-between" for God and God's people. In Jesus' time, priests were responsible for performing sacrifices that made atonement for sins and put people in a right relationship with God.

- A **king** is the ruler of a nation or group of people.

Read the following Scriptures, which Christians often identify as promises of the Messiah. Put a "P" next to Scriptures that seem to indicate hopes for a prophet; a "PR" next to those that seem to indicate hopes for a priest; and a "K" next to those that seem to indicate hopes for a king. (See the Answer Key on page 20).

___ **Deuteronomy 18:15-18**

___ **2 Samuel 7:12-16**

___ **Psalm 110**

___ **Isaiah 50:4-9**

___ **Ezekiel 34:15-16, 23-24**

___ **Micah 5:2-5a**

> **DAY 6: Ephesians 1:17-23**
> Paul says that we only come to understand what we're hoping for in Christ gradually, as we are guided by the Spirit. How has your understanding of hope developed over your life of faith? When and where have you witnessed the "immeasurable greatness" of God's power (verse 19)?

▰ Based on what you know about Jesus, how, would you say, did he fulfill messianic hopes for a prophet, a priest, and a king?

_____

_____

Great Expectations

The angel tells Joseph about God's great hope for the baby Jesus: "He will save his people from their sins" (**Matthew 1:21**). Other Scriptures about Jesus' birth, childhood, and youth also tell us about the expectations people held for the baby born in Bethlehem. Read the following Scriptures and then try paraphrasing them, or writing them in your own words to tell what the character(s) in each expect of Jesus.

Week One: God's Gift of Hope

Joy Peace Hope Love Joy Peace Hope Love Joy Peace

- Matthew 2:1-6

- Luke 1:26-33

- Luke 1:46-55

- Luke 1:67-79

- Luke 2:25-38

- Luke 3:15-16

- Based on what you know about Jesus, how did he meet these "great expectations"?

Option: Consider acting out these Scriptures, either as brief skits or pantomimes. Record your performances on video so that others can view them.

High Hopes

- When you were growing up, what hopes did you have for your life? Which of these hopes do you still have?

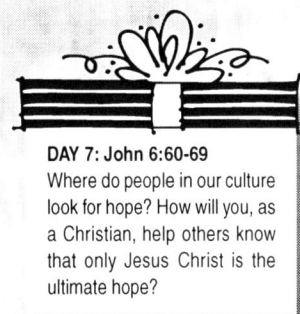

DAY 7: John 6:60-69
Where do people in our culture look for hope? How will you, as a Christian, help others know that only Jesus Christ is the ultimate hope?

- When you were growing up, what hopes did your parents, guardians, or other adults have for your life? Which of these hopes do they still have?

- What hopes, do you think, does God have for your life? What are you doing to realize those hopes today?

Shining With God's Light

God's gift of hope in Jesus Christ is a Christmas gift that won't break!

Divide into groups of three or four. In your groups discuss the questions on the following page. Work together to come up with ideas to which you can commit. Record these ideas in the space provided.

Week One: God's Gift of Hope

➤ **What gift will you give this Christmas that will bring someone else God's gift of hope?** Perhaps you and your youth group could collect gifts or money for a charity such as the Heifer Project (*www.heifer.org*). Gifts of animals and agricultural supplies given through Heifer International's "gift catalog"—from trees to water buffalo!—help people in underdeveloped countries become self-reliant, leading to a future filled with hope.

➤ **What gift will you ask for this Christmas that will help you be a giver of hope?** Perhaps you could ask for a book of devotionals from a classic or contemporary Christian author. It is difficult to share hope with others when our individual hopes are low. Reading and reflecting on fellow believers' insights can keep us aware of God's presence and power in the world and in our lives, rekindling and increasing our Christian hope.

Answers to Jesus' Job Description: *Deuteronomy 18:15-18-P; 2 Samuel 7:8-16-K; Psalm 110-PR, K; Isaiah 50:4-9-P; Isaiah 53:4-6-PR; Ezekiel 34:15-16, 23-24-K; Micah 5:1-5a-K*

WEEK TWO:
God's Gift of Love

LUKE 2:15-20

Reflecting on God's Light

When the angels had left them and gone into heaven, the shepherds said to one another, "Let us go now to Bethlehem and see this thing that has taken place, which the Lord has made known to us." So they went with haste and found Mary and Joseph, and the child lying in the manger. When they saw this, they made known what had been told them about this child; and all who heard it were amazed at what the shepherds told them. But Mary treasured all these words and pondered them in her heart. The shepherds returned, glorifying and praising God for all they had heard and seen, as it had been told them.

—Luke 2:15-20

DAILY BIBLE READINGS

Commit to reading, reflecting on, and praying about one of the devotional readings each day during the coming week.

DAY 1: Romans 5:6-11
"Peace on earth, and mercy mild, God and sinners reconciled." What's the connection between Christmas and Easter? How do the death and resurrection of Jesus allow us to understand fully the birth of Jesus?

What Do You Want for Christmas? (Part 2)

For one wild Christmas in the 1980's, American kids wanted dolls. Of course dolls were not new to kids' Christmas wish lists; dolls have been around a long time. In fact, archaeologists believe the world's oldest toy is a doll: a carved wooden figure with curly hair, unearthed on the Mediterranean island of Pantelleria. Dating back some four thousand years, it's been dubbed the "Barbie of the Bronze Age."

But during the 1983 holiday season, one particular doll was definitely in high demand. The Cabbage Patch Kids are, for many people, still icons of the whole decade. Introduced in 1982, these dolls were soft, chubby little figures with oddly large, puffy, plastic heads—and no two were exactly alike. Children seemed to fall in love with the "Kids" at first sight, even as cynical older siblings and adults insisted the dolls were ugly. One stubborn urban legend says the dolls were created as a late Cold War-era plan to get Americans used to what we'd all look like after exposure to nuclear fallout!

As it turns out, the real ugliness wasn't in the dolls. A cover of *Newsweek* in December 1983 proclaimed the Cabbage Patch Kids a

Christmas Gifts That Won't Break

"craze" and a "Christmas fad"—but that was an understatement. According to the official Cabbage Patch Kids website, some three million dolls had been sold by year's end, "but demand [had] not been met. The Cabbage Patch Kids Toys [went] on record as the most successful new doll introduction in the history of the toy industry." The dolls proved so successful and so scarce that Christmas, some parents (and likely more than a few opportunistic collectors) seemed to stop at nothing to get them. An issue of *Time* from the same month described a few of the more dramatic—and disgraceful—shenanigans. In one West Virginia department store, five thousand shoppers nearly rioted. In Pennsylvania, a crowd of one thousand waited eight hours for a store to open, only to become so violent that one woman broke her leg, four other people were injured, and the manager felt forced to defend himself with a baseball bat.

At their most basic level, dolls have no function other than to be objects of kids' affection. They exist to be loved and to help their "mommies" and (yes) "daddies" learn how to show love. So it's more than ironic that Cabbage Patch Kids inspired so much unlovable behavior.

God created us to give and receive love. From the very beginning, when Adam fell head over heels for Eve at first sight, calling her "bone of my bones and flesh of my flesh" (**Genesis 2:23**), we've been created for loving relationships. So why do we, as the human race and as individuals, do so many unlovable things? God's will for our lives sounds so simple—love God and love your neighbor (see **Matthew 22:37-39**)—but it proves to be so difficult. Each day offers us countless opportunities to act in loving ways, but for each one we take, we turn down at least two more. The prophet Isaiah lamented, "We have all become like one who is unclean, and all our righteous deeds are like a filthy cloth" (**Isaiah 64:6a**). We read the apostle Paul's beautiful words about true love—love that is patient and kind, that doesn't insist on its own way, love that never ends (see **1 Corinthians 13:4-7**)—and we know that what we usually call love doesn't measure up. What's wrong with us? Why do we lose that primal, childlike, innocent instinct to love and become, in some way, one more rioting shopper, fighting everyone else off in a crazed, selfish quest for what we want?

Angels told the shepherds in the fields, "[T]o you is born this day ...a Savior, who is the Messiah, the Lord" (**Luke 2:11**). And when the shepherds went to Bethlehem, what did they find? An image so simple yet so significant that it has remained one of the most commonly seen Christmas images, competition from snowmen and Santas notwithstanding: "Mary and Joseph, and the child lying in the manger" (**2:16**). New parents caring for their baby—an ordinary scene, one that takes place hundreds of thousands of times around the world each day. But "what had been told" the shepherds about this scene, about this child, was extraordinary, and "all who heard it were amazed" (**2:17-18**). This scene of love was a sign of salvation (see **2:12**). Mary and Joseph were caring for the One who cares for all; the baby in the manger embodied, as his uncle Zechariah said, "the tender mercy of our God" (**1:78**).

The power of sin stains even our best efforts to love God and one another. But in Jesus Christ, a greater power has arrived. The letter to Titus, in verses often read in worship at Christmas, declares, "[T]he grace of God has appeared, bringing salvation to all.... [Jesus] gave himself for us that he might redeem us from all iniquity and purify for himself a people of his own who are zealous for good deeds" (**Titus 2:11, 14**). We can be saved from sin and learn how to truly love—all because God, in Jesus, has first loved us. When we welcome him and believe in him, Jesus gives us "power to become children of God" (**John 1:12**): reconnected with the divine love that created us, and renewed in our ability to freely receive and give that love.

DAY 2: Deuteronomy 7:7-8
People sometimes act as though God spent the entire Old Testament being angry, and only became loving once Jesus was born. How does the Bible itself disprove this idea? How is God's history with ancient Israel one long love story?

What else could we want for Christmas, when God offers us so great a love?

Gathering in God's Light

Leader: You will need an Advent Wreath and a lighter. Select several youth to read aloud this opening liturgy.

READER 1: At Christmas time, we hear a lot about love …

READER 2: Well, open it, open it already! I know you're gonna love it!

READER 3: I just love hot chocolate and fresh-baked gingerbread!

READER 4: Hey—we're standin' under the mistletoe! Must be love …

READER 1: At Christmas time, we hear a lot about love …

Week Two: God's Gift of Love

READER 2: I know we're supposed to "love our fellow man" at Christmas... but what if "my fellow man" is that guy?

READER 3: I hate the way my family pretends to love one another at Christmas—we can hardly stand one another the rest of the year.

READER 4: I got a lot of presents... but I don't feel like I got any love.

<u>*Light two Advent candles.*</u>

READER 1: As the heavens are high above the earth, so great is God's steadfast love toward those who honor him (see **Psalm 103:11**).

DAY 3: Song of Solomon 8:6-7
Through the centuries, many biblical interpreters have read the Song of Solomon as a love song between God and God's people. How is Jesus Christ "a seal" of God's love for us? What do these verses teach us about the love that God offers?

READER 2: "I am the LORD your God, the Holy One of Israel, your Savior.... You are precious in my sight,... and I love you" (**Isaiah 43:3-4**).

READER 3: "God's love was revealed among us in this way: God sent his only Son into the world so that we might live through him" (**1 John 4:9**).

READER 4: "The life I now live... I live by faith in the Son of God, who loved me and gave himself for me" (**Galatians 2:20**).

One or all pray:

Holy God,
Even when we have not loved you or
   one another,
you have never stopped loving us.
May we celebrate, with wonder and joy,
   the gift of love you gave in your Son,
   Jesus Christ;
and in the strength of his Spirit may we live loving lives of service to our
   neighbors and to you.
This we pray in Jesus' name. Amen.

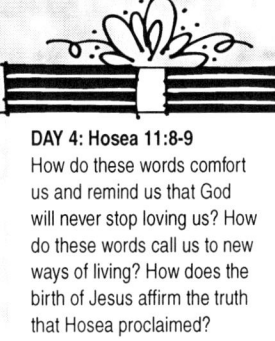

DAY 4: Hosea 11:8-9
How do these words comfort us and remind us that God will never stop loving us? How do these words call us to new ways of living? How does the birth of Jesus affirm the truth that Hosea proclaimed?

ALL: God's gift of love in Jesus Christ is the same yesterday, today, and forever! (based on **Hebrews 13:8**)

Share signs and words of peace with one another.

Reflecting on God's Light

Read **Luke 2:15-20**. Then read or listen to "What Do You Want for Christmas? Part 2" (page 22 or *abingdonyouth.com*). Discuss some or all of the following questions.

- What Christmas toy crazes can you recall?

- To what lengths will people go to get popular toys and electronics that are in short supply?

Week Two: God's Gift of Love

- How does our obsession with receiving certain items for Christmas keep us from showing God's love to one another during the Advent season?

- In what ways have you seen God's love at work so far this Advent season?

Responding to God's Light

 Leader: Choose one or more of the following activities and discussion starters.

Defining Our Terms

- What does the word *love* mean?
- How do we use the word *love* in our culture?

Look again at the Bible verses about love quoted in the Advent candle ritual (see **Psalm 103:11; Isaiah 43:3-4; 1 John 4:9; Galatians 2:20**). What makes the Bible's idea of love different from other ways we understand love?

New Faces at the Manger

Jesus was born to show us God's love and to save us with God's love. Too often, though, traditional images of his birth don't effectively communicate this truth. Not only have the usual images grown too familiar—the angels, the shepherds, the animals in the stable—but also the fact that Jesus is (obviously!) an infant in the Christmas story can keep us from remembering that his mission was to grow up and to give his life in love for us.

Choose one or more of the following New Testament figures, all of whom are people whose lives were changed by Jesus' love. Read their stories in Scripture. Now imagine that these people could travel back in time to be present at Jesus' birth. How, do you think, would they react? What would they do? What would they say—to the Christ Child, to his parents, even to us today?

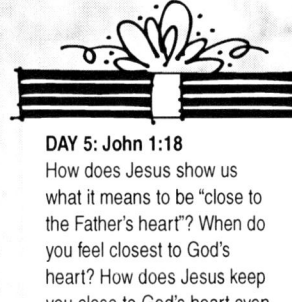

DAY 5: John 1:18
How does Jesus show us what it means to be "close to the Father's heart"? When do you feel closest to God's heart? How does Jesus keep you close to God's heart even when you don't "feel" it?

Assume the character of one of these biblical persons and, at the bottom of the page, create a short monologue about his or her thoughts and feelings at the manger.

- A man with a skin disease: **Mark 1:40-45**
- A small child: **Mark 10:13-16**
- The widow of Nain: **Luke 7:11-17**
- The woman at Simon's home: **Luke 7:36-50**
- Zacchaeus: **Luke 19:1-10**
- The repentant criminal: **Luke 23:39-43**
- A woman caught in adultery: **John 8:1-11**
- Lazarus and/or his sisters, Mary and Martha: **John 11:17-44**
- Simon Peter: **John 21:15-19**

Week Two: God's Gift of Love

Picturing Love

Leader: You will need old magazines, newspapers, and images printed from the Internet.

First Corinthians 13 is one of the best-known yet least understood descriptions of love in the world. Many people know this Scripture because they have heard it read at weddings. But many people *don't* know that the apostle Paul was talking more about God's love for us than our love for one another. Of course Paul wants his readers to love one another, but the love he describes is God's great love that makes all other loves possible.

Read **1 Corinthians 13** several times. Use images from old magazines and newspapers, printed from the Internet, and/or your drawings to illustrate Paul's "love chapter." Include images that illustrate both God's love for us and ways we can love one another. Display your work where others can see it during the Advent and Christmas seasons.

> **DAY 6: John 13:31-35**
> We don't fully receive God's gift of love in Jesus until we love others as Jesus loved us. What acts of love will you do this Christmas season that will let "everyone know that you are [one of Christ's] disciples"?

Love Feast

One way to show and share love with others is by eating together. The early church "broke bread at home and ate their food with glad and generous hearts" (**Acts 2:46**) as one expression of their love for God and for one another. These *agape* meals (the Greek word for self-giving love) were often connected with a celebration of the Lord's Supper (Communion). In the eighteenth century, the Moravian Church renewed this practice, calling it the "lovefeast." The lovefeast consists of simple food and beverages, provided by the community of believers—but not for themselves alone. Members invite, encourage, and warmly welcome visitors to share the food and the fellowship.

DAY 7: John 15:12-17
Jesus said the greatest love is to lay down one's life for one's friends. Jesus laid down his life for you. How often do you think of yourself as Jesus' beloved friend? How can you increasingly think of yourself this way during this Christmas season? How will thinking of others in this way shape your relationships this Christmas season?

Help your class or youth group plan a lovefeast during the Christmas season to which you can invite family, friends, and visitors. Include seasonal food and drink—hot apple cider and sweet rolls, for example—but keep the menu simple. Sing Christmas carols; the lovefeast is known as a musical event. Suggest conversation starters that will encourage participants to share with one another their positive memories and experiences of Christmas. For example: "What's your favorite Christmas song, and why?" "What's the best Christmas present you ever received?" "What one Christmas tradition would you absolutely not want to miss?" Above all, practice Christian hospitality by creating a welcoming, nonthreatening event at which the only expectation of your guests is their time and companionship.

Shining With God's Light

*God's gift of love in Jesus Christ is a
Christmas gift that won't break!*

What gift will you give this Christmas that will bring someone else God's gift of love? Maybe you're thinking about giving music to some of the people on your list. Why not give them some music by Christian artists that will communicate the message of God's love in Jesus? The Christmas season offers some natural possibilities, as many mainstream "secular" artists will release holiday albums that include traditional hymns and carols of faith. But you don't have to limit yourself to Christmas music. Such websites as *www.ccmusic.org* feature tools to help you find Christian music in almost every musical style imaginable, from hard rock to children's music. Fill up your friend's iPod with tunes that proclaim the good news of God's love!

What gift will you ask for this Christmas that will help you be a giver of love? Maybe you'll ask for diapers and baby blankets—no, not for yourself! You can then "re-gift" these and other items to Church World Service (CWS) as part of their Baby Kits— essential items that mothers need to care for their newborns in parts of the world stricken by extreme poverty or natural disaster. See CWS' complete list, so you know what to add to your list, at *http://www.churchworldservice.org/*.

WEEK THREE:
God's Gift of Joy

MATTHEW 1:22-25

Reflecting on God's Light

All this took place to fulfill what had been spoken by the Lord through the prophet:

"Look, the virgin shall conceive and bear a son,
and they shall name him Emmanuel,"
which means, "God is with us."

When Joseph awoke from sleep, he did as the angel of the Lord commanded him; he took her as his wife, but had no marital relations with her until she had borne a son; and he named him Jesus.

—*Matthew 1:22-25*

DAILY BIBLE READINGS

Commit to reading, reflecting on, and praying about one of the devotional readings each day during the coming week.

DAY 1: Psalm 100
What reasons does the psalm-singer give for "making a joyful noise" to God? What reasons would you add? What does your "joyful noise" sound like?

What Do You Want for Christmas? (Part 3)

During the 1996 Christmas season, lots of little kids wanted a furry red monster who laughed uncontrollably when squeezed. Tyco's "Tickle Me Elmo" was arguably the decade's most memorable holiday present. It was the 90's version of the Cabbage Patch Kids: a toy that inspired fierce devotion among its target audience (in this case, the preschool *Sesame Street* viewership), equally fierce loathing among cynics (the doll has been parodied in several places, including on *The Simpsons*), and ugly outbursts of violence among grown-ups desperate to buy it for their children. Robert Waller, a Wal-Mart clerk in Fredericton, New Brunswick, got manhandled by a crowd of some three hundred late-night shoppers two weeks before Christmas. He told *People* magazine, "I was pulled under, trampled—the crotch was yanked out of my brand-new jeans...I was kicked with a white Adidas before I became unconscious." Waller suffered damage to his back, a broken rib, a concussion, and several other injuries.

Such scenes were certainly a far cry from the ones that had inspired the toy's creation. Its inventor, Ron Dubren, first thought of the toy when he saw two children tickling each

Christmas Gifts That Won't Break

other and laughing themselves silly. He wanted to design a toy that could re-create what Dubren called a "feeling of utter hilarity." The runaway success of "Tickle Me Elmo" doesn't just say a lot about the popularity of a particular Muppet on TV, then—it also says a lot about our desire to recapture an innocent experience of pure joy.

What is *joy,* anyway? We commonly use the word as a synonym for "happiness" or "gladness"; but, for Christians, joy is something much more powerful. Joy was certainly powerful for C.S. Lewis, the Oxford professor and author of the famous children's fantasy series, *The Chronicles of Narnia.* When Lewis wrote his autobiography, he titled it *Surprised by Joy*—because real joy, for him, catches a person off guard. It is not an experience we can plan; instead, joy comes unexpectedly. Lewis writes:

> Joy (in my sense) has...one characteristic, and one only, in common with [happiness and pleasure]; the fact that anyone who has experienced it will want it again...I doubt whether anyone who has tasted it would ever, if both were in his power, exchange it for all the pleasures in the world. But then Joy is never in our power and pleasure often is.

A toy such as "Tickle Me Elmo" might re-create "utter hilarity," but real joy never can be captured in an object—it can only be lived. Joy arrives as a gift from somewhere outside ourselves—more accurately, it arrives from someone outside ourselves. Christians believe that this someone is the One whom the evangelist Matthew identifies as "Emmanuel," which means "God is with us" (**Matthew 1:23**). Our longing for joy is actually our longing for God. God answered that longing, once and for all, with the birth of a baby in Bethlehem.

The truth that God is with us is the reason the authors of Scripture can, again and again, call us to rejoice, even when circumstances appear to be less than joyful.

So many of our culture's Christmas celebrations emphasize feeling merry. If your local radio market has (as mine has) a 24-7 holiday music station from Thanksgiving (or even earlier!) through December 25, you've likely heard more than your fair share of up-tempo summons to rock around the Christmas tree, go walking in a winter wonderland, and have a holly, jolly Christmas. Even in the best of times, the merriment can become grating. If you're facing emotionally tough times during the holidays, it can feel like a slap in the face.

Biblical calls to rejoice, however, are nothing like our culture's incessant urging to strike up another chorus of "fa-la-la-la-la." Christians know that life can be difficult. We do not deny the reality of darkness in our world and in our individual lives. But because God is with us, we can joyfully profess, "The light shines in the darkness, and the darkness can never extinguish it" (**John 1:5**, NLT).

We tend to forget, in our Christmas Eve services of candlelight and carols, that the story of Jesus' birth takes place in great darkness. Considering first-century Jewish marriage customs, Joseph likely was in his early twenties, and Mary was almost certainly a young teenager. These two kids were far from home, coping with an oppressive imperial edict and an impending baby all at the same time. No one can offer them lodging for the night, and they can find no place to lay their newborn but in an animal's feeding trough. The first well-wishers are shepherds—folks who were not exactly considered high-class society during that time. And, before too long, King Herod is out for the baby's blood.

That's definitely not the Christmas story that Hallmark slaps on greeting cards! That's not even the Christmas story that churches from coast to coast lead their young children to act out in too-big robes and cardboard crowns. It's a dark story—but in its midst and at its heart, the light of God's love shines—the light of "good news of great joy for all the people" (**Luke 2:10**, emphasis added). Whether or not we feel joyful at Christmas, God is with us. "Rejoice in the Lord always," wrote the apostle Paul, "again I will say, Rejoice. ... The Lord is near" (**Philippians 4:4, 5**).

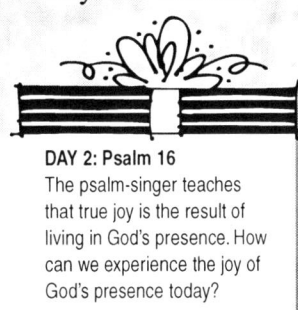

DAY 2: Psalm 16
The psalm-singer teaches that true joy is the result of living in God's presence. How can we experience the joy of God's presence today?

What else could we want for Christmas, when God offers us so great a cause for joy?

Gathering in God's Light

Leader: You will need an Advent Wreath and a lighter. Select several youth to read aloud this opening liturgy.

READER 1: At Christmas time, we hear a lot of joyful sounds ...

READER 2: (*sing*) "Just hear those sleigh bells jingling, ting-ting-tingling, too ..."

READER 3: (*sing*) "Follow me in merry measure, fa-la-la, fa-la-la, fa-la-la!"

Week Three: God's Gift of Joy

READER 4: (*sing*) "Oh, what fun it is to ride in a one horse open sleigh!"

READER 1: At Christmas time, we hear we're supposed to be joyful ...

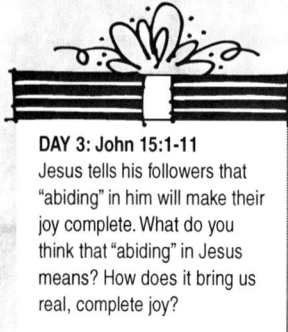

DAY 3: John 15:1-11
Jesus tells his followers that "abiding" in him will make their joy complete. What do you think that "abiding" in Jesus means? How does it bring us real, complete joy?

READER 2: ... but I feel upset and angry because my family has no money to spend on Christmas this year.

READER 3: ... but I feel sad and scared because this is our first Christmas since Mom died.

READER 4: ... but I just don't feel much of anything—I mean, it's just another day on the calendar, right?

Light three Advent candles.

READER 1: "Those who go out weeping ... shall come home with shouts of joy" (**Psalm 126:6**).

READER 2: "The people who walked in darkness have seen a great light; those who lived in a land of deep darkness—on them light has shined" (**Isaiah 9:2**).

READER 3: "Do not be afraid; for see—I am bringing you good news of great joy for all the people: to you is born this day in the city of David a Savior, who is the Messiah, the Lord" (**Luke 2:10-11**).

READER 4: "Rejoice in the Lord always; again I will say, Rejoice. ...The Lord is near" (**Philippians 4:4, 5**).

One or all pray:

None other is like you, O God:
   seated on high, yet looking far down
   to raise the poor from the dust and the
   needy from the ashes.
Please prepare us:
   for glad music when all is grim silence;
   for bright light when all is deep darkness;
   for the good news of the great joy of the birth of Emmanuel—
   God With Us, now and always.
This we pray in Jesus' name. Amen.

> **DAY 4: 1 Peter 1:8-9**
> What is the connection between believing in God and experiencing joy? How difficult do you find believing in God "whom you do not see"? How can the promise of "the salvation of your soul" sustain you in the face of doubt?

ALL: God's gift of joy in Jesus Christ is the same yesterday, today, and forever! (based on **Hebrews 13:8**)

Share signs and words of peace with one another.

Reflecting on God's Light

Read **Matthew 1:22-25**. Then read or listen to "What Do You Want for Christmas? Part 3" (page 34 or *abingdonyouth.com*). Discuss some or all of the following questions:

- What Christmas gifts have given you the most happiness?
- What Christmas songs and traditions emphasize joy?

Week Three: God's Gift of Joy

- What parts of the Christmas story in Scripture don't seem joyous at all?

- What is the difference between happiness and joy?

- How does the birth of Jesus bring us joy?

Responding to God's Light

 Leader: Choose one or more of the following activities and discussion starters.

Defining Our Terms

- What does the word *joy* mean?
- How do we use the word *joy* in our culture?

Look again at the Bible verses about joy quoted in the Advent candle ritual (see **Psalm 126:6; Isaiah 9:2; Luke 2:10-11; Philippians 4:4, 5**). What makes the Bible's concept of joy different from other ways we understand joy?

Echoes of Joy

Writer C.S. Lewis believed that we could find hints or "echoes" of joy in nature and in art.

- What in the natural world brings you joy?

Christmas Gifts That Won't Break

▪ What movies, music, TV shows, and books have given you a feeling like joy?

▪ How can these experiences be reminders for you of the source of true joy: Jesus Christ?

Breaking News of Great Joy

An angel brought "good news" (*gospel* means "good news") "of great joy" to the shepherds that first Christmas (**Luke 2:10**). When you receive good news, how do you tell this news to others? Maybe you pick up (or flip open) a phone; maybe you text or "tweet"; maybe you update your status on a social-networking site. Maybe you even send a letter (remember those?). Or, maybe you just shout the glad tidings to whomever's around to hear!

> **DAY 5: Psalm 126**
> Remember a time when your "mouth was filled with laughter." How will the memory of that time sustain you in more difficult times?

Luke tells us that the shepherds told anyone and everyone their good news (see **2:17-18**). Just for fun, imagine that the shepherds had at their disposal some of our modern technology. Working in groups of three or four, imagine yourself in one of the situations listed on page 42 and communicate the good news of Jesus' birth using one of the suggested techniques. Create a skit illustrating how you would spread the good news in this way or write in the space at the top of the next page what you would write on a postcard or post on a social-networking site.

Week Three: God's Gift of Joy

- A shepherd who is writing a note on a postcard for the next day's mail pickup
- A shepherd who is texting his friends or posting updates on Twitter (Remember, text messages can include no more than 160 characters; "tweets" can include no more than 140.)
- A shepherd who is updating his status on Judea's most popular social-networking site, Flockbook.com
- A shepherd who is being interviewed by a reporter for BNN (Bethlehem News Network)
- A shepherd who is holding a press conference
- A shepherd with a microphone or megaphone
- Any other creative communication technique you can think of!

> **DAY 6: Isaiah 35:8-10**
> Isaiah envisions the day when God will bring "everlasting joy" to God's people. Try to picture God's holy highway in your mind. What does it look like? Who is traveling on it? Where does it lead?

After you've "broken the good news" of Jesus' birth, think (and talk) about this question: *How will your youth ministry and/or congregation find equally creative ways to proclaim the gospel (good news) during this Christmas season and in the New Year?*

In the space below, make notes about any plans you and your group will want to follow up on in the weeks ahead.

Mary's Joys—and Ours

Leader: *You will need drawing paper, colored paper, markers, beads, string, and pens or pencils.*

In Europe during the Middle Ages, a popular subject for Christian devotion was "the seven joys of the Virgin Mary": seven events in Jesus' life that brought joy to his mother. Although the seven events chosen sometimes varied, one commonly found list was:

- The Annunciation (the announcement of Jesus' birth—**Luke 1:26-38**)
- The Birth of Jesus (**Luke 2:1-7**)
- The Wise Men Worship Jesus (**Matthew 2:1-12**)
- The Healing Miracles of Jesus (all four Gospels)
- The Resurrection of Jesus (all four Gospels)
- The Ascension of Jesus (**Acts 1:6-14**)
- The Sending of the Holy Spirit at Pentecost (**Acts 2:1-4**)

Week Three: God's Gift of Joy

Choose one of these traditional "seven joys" and, working individually or in small groups, create a response that communicates how it can bring us joy today. Illustrate it—draw a comic strip of the story or create a mosaic using small pieces of colored construction paper. Adapt the story as a dramatic monologue or a skit, or write a song about the story.

Next, in the space below, write your personal list of "seven joys"—perhaps seven people and things in your life that bring you joy; or seven moments from your past in which you sensed God was with you. Use string and beads to make a prayer rope or bracelet, with each bead (perhaps of different colors) representing one of these seven "joys" for which you can give thanks to God.

My Seven Joys

Closer Than Breath

In one of his sermons, the Rev. Dr. Martin Luther King, Jr., when describing the presence of the Holy Spirit, quoted the poet Alfred Lord Tennyson: "Closer is He than breathing, and nearer than hands and feet." When the apostle Paul tells us, "The Lord is near" (**Philippians 4:5**), that's how near the Lord is!

One form of prayer that can help us remember just how close Christ is to us—closer than our own breath—is the "breath prayer." Breath prayers are short, simple phrases, or even single words, repeated (silently) to the rhythm of inhaling and exhaling. Spend some time now, and in the coming week, trying this breath prayer: (*as you inhale*) "Rejoice in the Lord always"; (*as you exhale*) "for the Lord is near." Try adapting other Bible verses as breath prayers, too. Breath prayers can help us remember that God is close to us all the time—surely a reason to rejoice.

> **DAY 7: Nehemiah 8:10**
> How does "the joy of the LORD" give you strength each day? In honor of the ancient Israelites, enjoy some sweet food and share some of your food with those who have none.

Shining With God's Light

God's gift of joy in Jesus Christ
is a Christmas gift that won't break!

What gift will you give this Christmas that will bring someone else God's gift of joy? As angels brought good news of great joy to the shepherds, you might help others receive the good news by providing Bibles for them. The American Bible Society's

Week Three: God's Gift of Joy

"World's Greatest Gift Catalog" (*https://give.americanbible.org/*) gives you and your youth ministry the opportunity to give Bibles to persecuted Christians, refugees, troops abroad, and other populations in need of individual copies of the Scriptures, as well as opportunities to help fund the completion of translations of the Bible into languages that have never before had them.

What gift will you ask for this Christmas that will help you be a giver of joy? Since, as we've learned this week, Christian joy is rooted in knowing that Jesus is near, you might consider asking for some small, simple object that will remind you of Jesus' constant presence. Former editor of Pockets magazine Janet Knight suggests "a candle or a small cross," something you can keep "in the locations where you spend most of your day." You could, of course, use such an object that you already possess; but asking for a new one as a Christmas gift might give it special emphasis as you head into a new year of developing your awareness of Christ's continuing presence.

WEEK FOUR: God's Gift of Peace

LUKE 2:8-14

Reflecting on God's Light

In that region there were shepherds living in the fields, keeping watch over their flock by night. Then an angel of the Lord stood before them, and they glory of the Lord shone around them, and they were terrified. But the angel said to them, "Do not be afraid; for see—I am bringing you good news of great joy for all the people; to you is born this day in the city of David a Savior, who is the Messiah, the Lord. This will be a sign for you: you will find a child wrapped in bands of cloth and lying in a manger. And suddenly there was with the angel a multitude of the heavenly host, praising God and saying,

> "Glory to God in the highest heaven,
> and on earth peace among those whom he favors!"

—Luke 2:8-14

What Do You Want for Christmas?
(Part 4)

During the first decade of the 2000's, lots of teens (and grown-ups) put games at the top of their holiday wish lists. Not just any games, though—video games.

In November 2005, Microsoft launched its hotly anticipated Xbox 360. Not to be outdone—and to similar excitement—Sony unveiled its Playstation 3 in time for the 2006 holiday season. Manhattan resident Angel Paredes, for example, spent three nights on a sidewalk outside a Madison Avenue store in order to be the first to buy the new gaming platform, and told reporters, "It was totally worth it."

The Nintendo Wii also debuted in 2006. It distinguished itself with a unique remote control dubbed the "Wiimote." The Wiimote allows players to enter and interact with various virtual environments through natural, intuitive movements. To play Wii Bowling, for instance, simply swing your "Wiimote" as you would a real bowling ball. (Just make sure it's strapped to your wrist so you don't strike the real TV set along with the virtual pins!) "Insanely popular from the get-go," writes Tor Thorsen of GameSpot, "the console was nearly impossible to find at

DAILY BIBLE READINGS

Commit to reading, reflecting on, and praying about one of the devotional readings each day during the coming week.

DAY 1: John 14:27
How is the peace that Jesus promises different from the peace the world can give? In what ways do we receive and share Jesus' peace?

Christmas Gifts That Won't Break

retailers during its first year on the market. Now that it's in ample supply, the Wii routinely trounces its competitors"—although, with other companies developing Wii-like systems (as of this writing, for instance, Xbox is planning "Project Natal," a controller-free gaming and entertainment system), we can expect the "console wars" to continue throughout many Christmas seasons to come.

What makes video game consoles so popular? Like other tech toys—from MP3 players to electronic readers—these systems appeal to us because they show off the human capacity for creation, our ability to dream and imagine. The past decade's video game systems allow us to access elaborate, fully realized "other worlds" like never before. And not just sci-fi or sword-and-sorcery worlds like those of *Halo, Mass Effect,* and *Final Fantasy*—game consoles can connect us to radically revised versions of "the real world." Remember *The Sims*? By 2002 this virtual simulator of such mundane goings-on as eating and drinking, making friends, and getting (and losing) a job had become the best-selling PC game of all time and was soon exported to various gaming consoles. Sports games, which have become an annual purchase for many gamers, have become increasingly detailed and lifelike, accurately and precisely depicting athletes, coaches, and stadiums. Some games simulating military conflicts also have become eerily realistic. *Slate Magazine* said that the game *Call of Duty: Modern Warfare 2* was such an accurate portrayal of war that the violence in the game "is not easy to perform or forget."

The ability to use technology to transport ourselves to other worlds and to get a taste of experiences that might otherwise be inaccessible to us is impressive and can be both educational and entertaining. But we need to think critically about the kinds of worlds that we're using our God-given imagination to dream up and immerse ourselves in. Are we creating worlds where we are free to indulge every whim, treating others as a means to getting what we want? Or, are we creating worlds where we strive for that which is good for everyone?

The shepherds in the Bethlehem fields may have thought they were dreaming (once the terror wore off) when they heard angels singing, "Glory to God in the highest heaven, and on earth peace among those whom he favors" (**Luke 2:14**). These messengers came from outside their everyday experience—and so did the message. Shepherds weren't exactly the upper crust of first-century Mediterranean society. Respectable people didn't want shepherds hanging around. They stank, for starters—watching over dirty, smelly sheep day after day and night after night will do that to a person! And since they had to work nights, shepherds couldn't stay home to protect their families—a hard reality that branded them with disgrace in their society. In addition to all that, shepherds routinely faced accusations that their flocks grazed on land where they had no right to be. Shepherds never found much favor in anyone's eyes. Yet they—and not the "respectable" folk—were the first to hear "good news of great joy" (**2:10**)—the birth of the Messiah!

The angels offered the shepherds a vision of a new world: a world of justice and peace, a world where they were no longer shoved aside but were welcomed into the fold of "those whom [God] favors" (**2:14**). "To you," the angel tells them, "to you—the different, the mistrusted, the feared, the marginalized—is born the Lord!"

Don't miss this—this is radical stuff! The angels sing of a world where our usual notions of winners and losers and of who's "in" and who's "out" are shaken more vigorously than you can shake your

Wiimote! The angels are singing about the same world Mary sang about earlier in Luke's Gospel: a world where God "has brought down the powerful from their thrones, and lifted up the lowly; [where God] has filled the hungry with good things, and sent the rich away empty" (**1:52-53**). No wonder the shepherds hurried to that stable—they wanted to live in that world. Leaving behind their flocks (and their livelihood) must have seemed "totally worth it."

> **DAY 2: Psalm 122**
> Spend time today in prayer not only for Jerusalem but also for all places in the world that do not know peace.

God has dreamed up a world of justice, a world at peace. And the "platform" by which we gain access to that world is "the child lying in the manger" (**2:16**)—the baby who would grow up to proclaim God's special blessing upon the merciful and the peacemakers (see **Matthew 5:7, 9**).

It's a world where God's fierce love "for all the people" (**2:10**) means that some of the people will be nudged out of their comfort and shaken out of their power and privilege. But it's a world where all the people will be at peace, for all the people will know that they are favored by God. As the prophet Isaiah foresaw, it's a world where people "will not hurt or destroy on all my holy mountain; for the earth will be full of the knowledge of the LORD as the waters cover the sea" (**Isaiah 11:9**).

What else could we want for Christmas, when God offers us such great peace?

Week Four: God's Gift of Peace

Gathering in God's Light

 Leader: You will need an Advent Wreath and a lighter. Select several youth to read aloud this opening liturgy.

READER 1: Christmastime is a time for peace...

READER 2: "Twas the night before Christmas, and all through the house, not a creature was stirring, not even a mouse..."

DAY 3: Isaiah 9:6-7
Christians have long read these verses as a prophecy about Jesus. Find and listen to a recording of "For Unto Us a Child is Born" from Handel's *Messiah*. As you do, reflect on what it means to worship Jesus as the "Prince of Peace."

READER 3: "I am sure that I have always thought of Christmas time...as a good time; a kind, forgiving, charitable, pleasant time; the only time I know of, in the long calendar of the year, when men and women seem by one consent to open their shut-up hearts freely." (from Charles Dickens' *A Christmas Carol*)

READER 4: "I heard the bells on Christmas Day their old, familiar carols play,

and wild and sweet the words repeat of peace on earth, goodwill to men!" — Henry Wadsworth Longfellow

READER 1: Christmastime is a time for peace...

READER 2: ... but our world is not at peace: Wars rage on around the globe, and acts of terror are a threat to every nation.

READER 3: Our society is not at peace: Those most in need of charity and kindness too often go without, and justice is still denied to the poor and the powerless.

READER 4: Our homes are not at peace: They are stirring with pain and mistrust, or resentment and anger, or violence and abuse.

DAY 4: Mark 9:50
Why, do you think, does Jesus compare being "at peace with one another" to salt? Make and share a salty snack with someone as an edible sign of your commitment to live in peace.

Light four Advent candles.

READER 1: "A child has been born for us, a son given to us; authority rests upon his shoulders; and he is named Wonderful Counselor, Mighty God, Everlasting Father, Prince of Peace" (**Isaiah 9:6**).

READER 2: "He delivers the needy when they call, the poor and those who have no helper. He has pity on the weak ... and saves the lives of the needy. From oppression and violence he redeems their life; and precious is their blood in his sight" (**Psalm 72:12-14**).

READER 3: "Do not worry about anything, but in everything by prayer and supplication with thanksgiving let your requests be made known to God. And the peace of God, which surpasses all understanding, will guard your hearts and your minds in Christ Jesus" (**Philippians 4:6-7**).

READER 4: "Peace I leave with you; my peace I give to you. I do not give to you as the world gives. Do not let your hearts be troubled, and do not let them be afraid" (**John 14:27**).

<u>*One or all pray:*</u>

Most High, you rule over all,
   and you command the nations to be still and know that you
   alone are God.
Speak your powerful word of peace today,
   that we and the world may truly know
   the freedom from chilling fear and freedom for loving service
   that is found by entrusting ourselves to your Son.
This we pray in Jesus' name. Amen.

ALL: **God's gift of joy in Jesus Christ is the same yesterday, today, and forever!** (based on **Hebrews 13:8**)

<u>*Share signs and words of peace with one another.*</u>

Reflecting on God's Light

Read **Luke 2:8-14**. Then read or listen to "What Do You Want for Christmas? Part 4" (page 48 or *abingdonyouth.com*). Discuss some or all of the following questions:

- In what ways are you at peace during the Advent and Christmas seasons?
- What parts of the Advent and Christmas seasons aren't very peaceful?

- The shepherds who first heard the good news of Jesus' birth were outcasts and misfits in their society. Who are some of the people who are ignored or left out in our society?
- How can we bring the peace of Christ to these people?

Responding to God's Light

Leader: Choose one or more of the following activities and discussion starters.

Defining Our Terms

- What does the word *peace* mean?
- How do we use the word *peace* in our culture?

Look again at the Bible verses about joy quoted in the Advent candle ritual (see **Isaiah 9:6; Psalm 72:12-14; Philippians 4:6-7; John 14:27**). What makes the Bible's idea of peace different from other ways we understand peace?

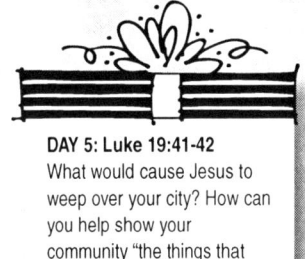

DAY 5: Luke 19:41-42
What would cause Jesus to weep over your city? How can you help show your community "the things that make for peace"?

Peace Puzzles

Leader: You will need Bibles, cardstock, scissors, and pens or pencils.

The Hebrew word for peace, *shalom*, literally means "health," "completeness," and "wholeness." In the New Testament, the Greek word for *peace* takes on some of this meaning as well. In groups of three or four, read and discuss some or all of the following Scriptures.

Week Four: God's Gift of Peace

How does each one describe or depict shalom? What divisions have been overcome? What do these Scriptures say about health and wholeness? Which of these Scriptures describe promises from God, which give us instructions to follow, and which do both?

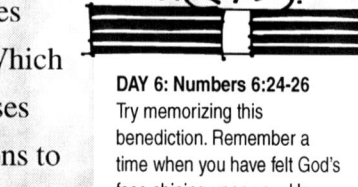

DAY 6: Numbers 6:24-26
Try memorizing this benediction. Remember a time when you have felt God's face shining upon you. How will your face reflect the peace of God for someone else today?

- **Leviticus 26:3-6**
- **Psalm 85**
- **Proverbs 10:10**
- **Proverbs 16:7**
- **Isaiah 54:9-10**
- **2 Corinthians 13:11-13**
- **Ephesians 2:13-18**

Then, with your group, choose one of the verses to write and/or illustrate on a piece of cardstock. Cut up your card as a jigsaw puzzle. Exchange puzzles with another group and put together one another's puzzles. This activity reminds us that *shalom* means taking something that is broken and making it whole.

Peace and the Poor

The prophets of the Bible teach that we cannot know peace in the world without justice. We must follow Jesus' example by reaching out to those who are poor, sick, hungry, oppressed, and ignored. Read the Scriptures on the next page. Each one looks at God's response to injustice. Beside each, describe where you see a similar problem of injustice in the world today.

📖 Isaiah 59:1-8: _____

📖 Jeremiah 6:13-20: _____

📖 Zechariah 7:8-12: _____

Individually, or as a group, contact a local elected official or federal representative about a specific issue of injustice that you identify. Inquire about his or her record on the issue and urge him or her to consider persons in need when voting on legislation and policy.

Pray for the Peace of ...

Leaders: Beforehand browse news sources to identify places of unrest around the world. Also bring sticky notes or thumbtacks, along with a globe or world map if there is not already one in your meeting space.

Psalm 122 calls on us to "Pray for the peace of Jerusalem" (verse 6). The city of Jerusalem's name derives from the word *shalom*; but, even today, peace has proved elusive there. Take time to reflect on other places in the world that need our prayers for peace. Mark these places on a map or globe with sticky notes or thumbtacks. Compile a list of these cities and countries and appoint one person to send this list to the rest of the group by e-mail, text message, or through a social-networking site. Use the list as a reminder to pray each day for these parts of the world.

DAY 7: Colossians 1:19-20
These verses remind us why Jesus' birth is worth celebrating: He was born to die, to make peace between God and all things "through the blood of his cross." Design a Christmas card that visually shares this truth.

Week Four: God's Gift of Peace

"Peace! Be Still!"

Read **Mark 4:35-41**. In the ancient world, natural storms were, understandably, powerful symbols of all the forms of chaos that threaten us. Jesus, however, is able to bring order and peace to all chaos.

As a group, read and reflect on this story using the practice of *lectio divina* ("divine" or "spiritual reading"). There is no "one right way" to do *lectio divina*; but here is one suggested method:

1. *Read the Scripture aloud a first time.* After a brief silence, identify the word, phrase, or image from the text that most attracts your attention. Spend some time meditating on that word, phrase, or image.

2. *Read the text aloud a second time.* After a brief silence, try to answer (silently) this question: Where do you see yourself in this story? What message, do you think, does Jesus want to give you through this Scripture?

3. *Read the text aloud a third time.* After a brief silence, try to answer (silently) this question: Based on your reading of and reflection on this Scripture, what is Jesus calling you to do or to be this day?

4. *Close with a prayer of thanksgiving* for your encounter with God's Word.

Work as a group to present a dramatization of this Bible story. If possible, videotape your performance and make it available for the congregation to view.

Blessed Are the Peacemakers

Jesus said, "Blessed are the peacemakers, for they will be called children of God" (**Matthew 5:9**).

- What does it mean to be a peacemaker?

- Based on what you know about peace from the Scriptures you've read and from the activities above, how would someone go about making peace?

As a group, identify someone in your congregation or community who acts as a peacemaker. This could be a person who brings hope to a neighborhood torn apart by violence; it could be a teacher or principal who is especially skilled at helping students work through conflicts; it could be someone who works vigorously to fight hunger or poverty; it could also be a person who demonstrates extraordinary grace and forgiveness. If you have trouble identifying someone, scan local news sources on the Internet.

Once you have chosen your local peacemaker, determine a way that you can honor this person. Some ideas are: creating a card or certificate, lifting up this person on your church website or blog, finding ways to tell other people in your congregation or community about this person's contributions, or making a donation in this person's honor to a cause that is important to him or her.

Shining With God's Light

*God's gift of peace in Jesus Christ is a
Christmas gift that won't break!*

▰ **What gift will you give this Christmas that will bring someone else God's gift of peace?** You could choose to support a charity that helps innocent victims of war. The HALO Trust, for example, is a charity devoted to "one of the most inherently dangerous jobs on earth," removing still-live landmines and other "debris of war" so that such devices no longer claim victims (*http://www.halousa.org/*).

▰ **What gift will you ask for this Christmas that will help you be a giver of peace?** Consider taking a cue from **Ephesians 6:15**: "As shoes for your feet put on whatever will make you ready to proclaim the gospel of peace." If footwear is on your Christmas wish list, why not ask for recycled shoes? They're out there—just check the Internet for options—and their purchase reduces your ecological footprint (literally!) and promotes the *shalom* of the environment. You might also ask for TOMS shoes. When someone purchases a pair of TOMS shoes, the company donates a pair to a child in need. (The shoes are also manufactured in factories that pay fair wages and "operate under sound labor conditions.")

BONUS:
Organize a Churchwide Advent Study

God's Gifts for All Ages

Christmas Gifts That Won't Break encourages people to experience God's gifts of hope, love, joy, and peace during the Advent season. These gifts never break! Material things wear out, break, erode, go out of fashion, and can be lost or stolen. We should build our happiness instead on things we cannot lose. A churchwide Advent program for all ages will help people learn more about the unbreakable gifts God offers through the birth of Jesus—gifts that give us more abundant life. The study offers opportunities for learning, for intergenerational projects and activities, and for reaching out to the community with hope, joy, love, and peace.

Schedule for a Churchwide Advent Study:

In addition to this book, you will need:

- *Christmas Gifts That Don't Break* by James W. Moore
- *Christmas Gifts That Don't Break for Children*

Many churches have weeknight programs that include an evening meal, an intergenerational gathering time, and separate classes for children, youth, and adults. The following schedule illustrates one way to organize a weeknight program.

- 5:30 P.M.: Gather for a meal.
- 6:00 P.M.: Intergenerational gathering that introduces the Advent gift (from James W. Moore's *Christmas Gifts That Don't Break*) and lighting an Advent candle. The time may include audiovisual presentations, skits, music, other presentations, and opening prayer.
- 6:15 P.M.–8:45 P.M.: Classes for children, youth, and adults

You may want to schedule the Advent study as a Sunday School program. This approach would be similar to the weeknight setting. The following schedule takes into account a shorter class time, which is common for Sunday morning programs.

- Intergenerational gathering that features the Advent gift (*10 minutes*)
- Classes for children, youth, and adults (*45 minutes*)

Choose a schedule that works best for your congregation and its existing Christian Education programs.

Advent Candle Lighting for Use in Worship Services

You may choose to use the prayers below (also in the Leader Guide) as part of lighting the Advent candle during worship.

First Sunday of Advent—The Gift of Hope

Leader: "The unbreakable gift for this first Sunday of Advent is the gift of hope."

Light the first candle.

Pray: "Dear God, thank you for the season of Advent and the gift of hope. Help us to prepare our hearts for your coming and to remember the true meaning of Christmas. Amen."

Second Sunday of Advent—The Gift of Love

Leader: "The unbreakable gift for this second Sunday of Advent is the gift of love."

Light two candles.

Pray: "Dear God, thank you for the gift of love. May we share this gift with others and learn how to love unconditionally. Help us during this Christmas season to practice love in action with family, friends, and strangers. Amen."

Third Sunday of Advent—The Gift of Joy

Leader: "The unbreakable gift for this third Sunday of Advent is the gift of joy."

Light three candles.

Pray: "Dear God, thank you for the gift of joy and for the way it brightens our days. Help us to give joy to others through what we say and do. Show us how to make this Christmas a true season of joy. Amen."

Fourth Sunday of Advent—The Gift of Peace

Leader: "The unbreakable gift for this fourth Sunday of Advent is the gift of peace."

Light four candles.

Pray: "Dear God, thank you for the gift of peace. Help us to put peace into practice in our lives and to show others the path to true peace. Remind us to serve as peacemakers and to share the love of God with those in need. Amen."